YOUR KNOWLEDGE HAS VALUE

Lea Kliem

Aus der Reihe: e-fellows.net stipendiaten-wissen

e-fellows.net (Hrsg.)

Band 423

Regulating Emotions: Five perspectives

GRIN Publishing

Bibliographic information published by the German National Library:

The German National Library lists this publication in the National Bibliography; detailed bibliographic data are available on the Internet at http://dnb.dnb.de .

Imprint:

Copyright © 2011 GRIN Verlag, Open Publishing GmbH
Print and binding: Books on Demand GmbH, Norderstedt Germany
ISBN: 978-3-656-18786-8

This book at GRIN:

http://www.grin.com/en/e-book/192865/regulating-emotions-five-perspectives

GRIN - Your knowledge has value

Since its foundation in 1998, GRIN has specialized in publishing academic texts by students, college teachers and other academics as e-book and printed book. The website www.grin.com is an ideal platform for presenting term papers, final papers, scientific essays, dissertations and specialist books.

Visit us on the internet:

http://www.grin.com/

http://www.facebook.com/grincom

http://www.twitter.com/grin_com

Emotion and Motivation

Regulating Emotions

Five Perspectives

Lea Kliem

Jacobs University Bremen

Spring 2011
May, 9, 2011
Word Count: 2044 words

Introduction

In a time where human kind has come to love to control every single aspect of live, sayings like "Control your emotion, or it will control you", gain relevance. But how does this process of gaining control through regulation work? And can one even speak about conscious 'control' through emotion regulation? Or is the process of emotion regulation rather a subconscious, automatic process? Looking at emotion regulation from five different perspectives, this paper provides an overview of the broad field of emotion regulation. As suggested by Cornelius (1995), the perspectives considered include the Darwinian, the Jamesian, the Cognitive and the Social Constructivist perspective. Additionally, as the field of neuroscience recently made some important contributions to emotion regulation, it is also considered in this paper as a fifth perspective.

Emotion regulation

Emotion regulation "refers to how we try to influence which emotions we have, when we have them, and how we experience and express these emotions" (Gross, 2008: 497). Although emotions play an important role in our life, when they occur at the wrong time, the wrong level of intensity or the wrong type, there may be a great motivation to regulate them (Gross, 2008). This regulation encompasses changing one or several aspects of emotion which may include "the eliciting situation, attention, appraisal, subjective experience, behavior, or physiology" (Bargh & Williams, 2007 and Gross & Thompson, 2007 in Mauss, Bunge & Gross, 2007). The result of such regulation may be diminishment or augmentation of an emotions amplitude or duration (ibid). It may also lead to a total suppression of an emotion (Gross, 2008). Although emotion regulation is often related to the turning down of experiential as well behavioral aspects of negative emotions, it may also refer to positive emotions (ibid). Unquestionable emotion regulation may refer to different processes. Categorized based on the point in time of the emotion-generative process they have their primary impact, Gross distinguishes between situation selection, situation modification, attentional deployment, cognitive change and response modulation (Gross, 2008). The first four of these processes are "antecedent- focused" as they take place before an emotion arises, while, contrasting, "response- focused" strategies may be utilized after an emotional response has been generated (ibid). Furthermore, researchers have distinguished between unconscious and conscious emotion regulation processes (Mayer & Salovey, 1995) as well as between automatic and controlled ones (Bargh & Williams, 2007).

Darwinian Perspective

Charles Darwin, often considered to be the founding father of emotion research, argued that emotions have been shaped by evolutionary pressures (Cornelius, 1995). Emotional expressions are thus remnants of once beneficial behavior (ibid). It therefore may be argued that emotions are regulated in a way, that only those emotions that over time proved to increase survival chances were passed on to future generations and are still prevalent today. According to Tooby and Cosmides the structure of the human past is reflected by our emotions (Tobb & Cosmides, 1990) and their regulation "should be beneficial to an individual's success of survival and fitness" (Calini, Ferri & Duman, 2009). There is some evidence that certain processes of emotion regulation have a genetic basis. Twin studies have produced evidence concerning the partial heritability of emotion regulation and molecular genetics have identified specific genes such as 5-HTTLPR, COMPT and MAOA to be associated with emotion regulation (ibid).

Furthermore, emotion regulation may take place through the regulation of facial expressions. According to the Darwinian Perspective there is a close link between emotions and expression and research has shown that emotional experiences correspond with the facial activity observed (Ekman, Friesen & Ancoli, 1980). According to McIntosh, "the ability of voluntary facial actions [...] indicate[s] that individuals can regulate their emotions by controlling their facial movements" (McIntosh, 1996: 19). The facial feedback hypothesis, which states that the control of expressions impacts the underlying emotion, should therefore be considered (Adelmann & Zajonc, 1989). According to Gross, this form of response modulation may not only amplify emotional experiences but may also cause emotions to be muted when facial activity is inhibited (Gross, 2008). Although this hypothesis could potentially also be classified as Jamesian, since Jamesians believe that facial actions as a type of bodily reaction can create an emotional state, it is the Darwinians that suggests that they may actually regulate emotions. Ekmanns and Friensen's 'Display rules' defined "as procedures learned early in life for the management of affect displays [...] prescribe what to do about the display of each affect in different social settings" may "deintensify, intensify, neutralize, or mask" facial expressions (Ekman, Sorenson, & Friesen, 1969:87). Although, Darwinians believe emotional expressions to be universal, 'Display rules' as such may vary across cultures.

Jamesian Perspective

The Jamesian perspective of emotion research focuses on automatic bodily changes including expressive behaviors, instrumental acts and physiological changes that directly follow the perception of an emotion triggering fact and create feelings (Cornelius, 1995). These feelings are equated with emotions (James, 1884 in Cornelius, 1995). The approach mainly focuses on visceral changes as well as changes in the autonomic nervous system (Cornelius, 1995) and research related to emotion regulation concentrates on 'response modulation' which "refers to influencing physiological, experiential, or behavioral responses relatively directly" (Gross, 2008: 504). Exercise, relaxation, physical touch or sleep may for example be used to decrease physiological and therewith experiential aspects of negative emotions (ibid, Gross & Feldman Barrett, 2011).

According to Gross and Levenson (1997), emotion regulation may have implications for physiological reactivity. However, what exact implication depends on the type of emotion regulation. Cognitive reappraisal, on which I will elaborate on later, has been found to lead to decreases (Gross & John, 2003) or increases (Mauss et al., 2007) in physiological activity while expressive suppression has consistently been found to lead to increases (Lam, Dickerson, Zoccola, & Zaldivar,2009). One study has for example shown that participants instructed to suppress their expressions while watching a disgusting film showed significant increases in sympathetic arousal, skin conductance and blood pressure (Gross & Levenson, 1993 in Calini, Ferri & Duman, 2009). However, the same study showed that this physiological change did not lead to a change in the emotion experienced (ibid). This not only contradicts the facial feedback hypothesis but is also incongruent with the Jamesian perspective, which would predict a change of one's feeling is response to the increase in sympathetic arousal.

Cognitive Perspective

Considering emotion regulation from a cognitive perspective, the concept of cognitive change is especially important (Ochnser & Gross, 2005). Cognitive theories, such as Magda Arnold's or Richard S. Lazarus appraisal theories based on peripheralist theories, claim that the different appraisals of bodily reactions lead to different emotions in such a way that appraisal outcomes predict emotional states (Cornelius, 1995). Cognitive change "refers to changing one or more of these appraisals in the way that alters the situation's emotional significance, by changing how one thinks either about the situation itself or about one's capacity to manage the demands it poses" (Gross, 2008: 503). The Lazarus- Zajonc debate revealed different understandings of the term appraisal (Cornelius, 1995). While Lazarus sees appraisal as a slow and deliberate cognitive process (Lazarus, 1982), Zajonc equates appraisal with fast and automatic affective reactions (Zajonc 1980). Reprisal, being one form of cognitive change refers to a change in appraisal as understood by Lazarus. According to Ochner and Gross, it involves "reinterpreting the meaning of a stimulus to change one's emotional response to it" (Ochsner & Gross, 2005: 245). This response occurs to changes either in internal or in external conditions and may "arise from new cues, reflection about the original evidence, or feedback from the effect of the individual's own reactions" (Defares, 1979: 124). Research has shown that reappraisal may lead to a decrease in negative emotion experiences as well as in expressive behavior (Gross, 1998). Furthermore, it does not require additional cognitive resources (Richards and Gross, 2000 in Calini, et al., 2009) and may lead to reduced cardiovascular responses (Calini, et al. 2009). Not to leave out Zajonc's understanding of appraisal, Mauss et al. introduced the concept of automatic emotion regulation (Mauss et al., 2007). Based on research that showed that when primed for a specific goal, unconscious goal pursuing may take place, automatic emotion regulation, they argue, happens unconsciously, without deliberate efforts to do so through the registration of sensory inputs which in turn activate the relevant knowledge structures that influence respective psychological functions (ibid).

Social Constructivist Perspective

The Social Constructivist Perspective sees emotions as social constructions that serve as transitory social roles, where roles are defined as "a socially prescribed set of responses to be followed by a person in a given situation" (Cornelius, 1995: 145). This implied that these roles are culturally determined and learned (Cornelius, 1995), through socialization early in infancy (Malatesta & Haviland, 1982) causing them to govern our emotional performances implicitly (Armon- Jones, 1986 & Averill, 1984 in Cornelius, 1995). Scholars following the social constructivist perspective have argued that emotion regulation fulfills a culture-dependent, social function (Fischer, Manstead, Evers, Timmers & Valk, 2004; Buttler & Gross, 2009) by leading us to 'appropriate' our feelings in social situations (Hochschild, 1979). This regulation of the expressive as well as experiential characteristics of emotions occurs through the internalization of 'feeling rules' that determine what is culturally appropriate to feel in a given situation (Hochschild, 1983). Laughing out loud or experiencing happiness in a funeral setting for example would be judged as inappropriate by most Westerners. Emotions may also be regulated through emotional re-education (Cornelius, 1995). Studies by Smith and Kleinman showed that medical students were able to eliminate feelings of disgust or sexual arousal when examining cadavers or patients after they had undergone emotional re-training (Smith & Kleinmann, 1989 in Cornelius 1995). Note how this can also be considered a form of cognitive change as it involves changing one's reappraisal of the situation. If no reappraisal, but instead emotion suppression takes place, negative social as well as consequences such as worse memory, decreased comfort for interaction partners and significantly less social support are likely to arise (Butler et al., 2003; Gross & John, 2003; Gross, 2008). The scope of those consequences however, is moderated by cultural values and may differ among cultures (Buttler, Lee & Gross, 2007). This cultural moderation can be seen as analogy to the concept of 'Display rules' mentioned earlier, which could be discussed in this section equally well.

Neuroscience Perspective

According to Panksepp, there is biological evidence for the existence of at least seven innate emotional systems within the brain of mammals, consisting of neural circuits that activate or inhibit motor subroutines and concurrent autonomic- hormonal changes and change sensory, perceptual and cognitive processing (Pankseepp, 1998). Acknowledging that "basic emotional processes emerge from homologous brain mechanisms" (Pankseepp, 1998: 51), the prefrontal cortex could be identified as the structure responsible for affective regulation (Coffey, 1987 cited in Stein, Leventhal, & Trabasso, 1990; Ochsner & Gross, 2008). Ochsner and Gross also found the dorsal and ventral portions of the anterior cingulated cortex activated during reappraisal (Ochsner & Gross, 2008). Additionally they found increases in the amygdala as well as the insula after receiving viscerosensory impulses (ibid). Similarly, a study by Levesque et al. (2003) found activation of the right orbitofrontal cortex and the lateral prefrontal cortex during conscious, voluntary reappraisal of sadness. The fact that different scholars have found activation in different regions of the cortex may be a result of weather participants were asked to reinterpret a situation or distract themselves from a stimulus (Ochsner & Gross, 2008).

Conclusion

In conclusions, there are many different understandings and forms of emotion regulation, but while as commonly believed some have to do with us taking control of our emotions, certainly not all do. Many unconscious, implicit and automatic emotion regulation processes influence the way we experience our own emotions and perceive those of others. Depending on our motivations and situational circumstances, we might choose to suppress expressive behavior and hide our emotions from others, therewith causing increases in the activation of our sympathetic nervous system or reappraise a situation with help of the prefrontal cortex. Cultural determinants may influence how and when we regulate our emotions as may personal characteristics. After all, virtually all emotions are regulated (Tomkins, 1984), and it has even been argued that emotions and their regulation should not be understood as separate phenomena (Kappas, 2011).

Bibliography

Adelmann, P. K., & Zajonc, R. B. (1989). Facial efference and the experience of emotion. *Annual Review of Psychology, 40,* 249-280.

Bargh, J. A., & Williams, L. E. (2007). The non-conscious regulation of emotion. Annual Review of Psychology. In J.J. Gross (Ed.), *Handbook of emotion regulation* (pp. 429- 445). New York: Guilford Press.

Butler, E. A., Lee, T. L., & Gross, J. J. (2007). Emotion regulation and culture: are the social consequences of emotion suppression culture-specific? *Emotion, 7*(1), 30-48.

Butler, E. A., & Gross, J. J. (2009). Emotion and Emotion Regulation: Integrating Individual and Social Levels of Analysis. *Emotion Review, 1*(1), 86-87.

Canli, T., Ferri, J., & Duman, E. A. (2009). Genetics of emotion regulation. *Neuroscience, 164*(1), 43-54.

Cornelius, R. R. (1995). *The Science of Emotion: Research and Tradition in the Psychology of Emotion* (p. 260). Prentice Hall.

Defares, P. B. (1979). Social Perception and Environmental Quality. *Urban Ecology, 4,* 119-137.

Ekman, P. Friesen, W. V., & Ancoli, S. (1980). Facial signs of emotional experience. *Journal of Personality and Social Psychology, 39,* 1125- 1134.

Ekman, P., Sorenson, E. R., Friesen, W. V. (1969). Pan- Cultural Elements in Facial Displays of Emotion. *Science, 164*(3875), 86-88.

Fisher, A., Manstead, A. S. R., Evers, C., Timmers, M., & Valk, G. (2004). Motives and Norms Underlying Emotion Regulation.*The regulation of emotion* (pp. 187-210).

Gross, J. J. (1998). The Emerging Field of Emotion Regulation: An Integrative Review. *Review of General Psychology, 2*(3), 271-299.

Gross, J. J. (2008). Emotion Regulation. In M. Lewis, M. Haviland-Jones, & L. F. Barrett (Eds.), *Handbook of emotions* (3rd ed., pp. 497-512). New York, NY: Guilford.

Gross, J. J. (2011). Emotion Generation and Emotion Regulation: One or two depends on your point of view. *Emotion Review, 3*(8), 8-16.

Gross, J. J., & John, O. P. (2003). Individual differences in two emotion regulation processes: Implications for affect, relationships, and well-being. *Journal of Personality and Social Psychology, 85,* 348–362.

Gross, J. J., & Levenson, R.W. (1997). Hiding feelings: the acute effects of inhibiting negative and positive emotion. *Journal of Abnormal Psychology, 106,* 95-103.

Hochschild, A. R. (1979). Emotion Work, Feeling Rules, and Social Structure. *The American Journal of Sociology, 85*(3), 551-575.

Hochschild, A. R. (1983). *The Managed Heart: Commercialization of Human Feeling*, Berkeley, CA: University of California Press.

Kappas, A. (2011). Emotion and Regulation are One! *Emotion Review, 3*(1), 17-25.

Malatesta, C. Z. & Haviland, J. M. (1982). Learning Display Rules: The Socialization of Emotion Expression in Infancy. *Child Development, 53*(4), 991-1003.

Mauss, I. B., Bunge, S. A., & Gross, J. J. (2007). Automatic Emotion Regulation. *Social and Personality Psychology Compass, 1*(1), 146-167.

Mauss, I. B., Cook, C. L., Cheng, J. Y. J., Gross, J. J. (2007). Individual differences in cognitive reappraisal: experiential and physiological responses to an anger provocation. *International Journal of Psychophysiology, 66*, 116- 124.

McIntosh, D. N. (1996). Facial Feedback Hypotheses: Evidence, Implications, and Directions. *Motivation and Emotion, 20*(2), 121- 147.

Lazarus, R. S. (1982). Thoughts on the relations between emotion and cognition. *American Psychologist, 46,* 819-834.

Lévesque, J., Eugène, F., Joanette, Y., Paquette, V., Mensour, B., Beaudoin, G., Leroux , J.-M., Bourgouin, P. & Beauregard, M. (2003). Neural circuitry underlying voluntary self-regulation of sadness, *Biological Psychiatry 53,* 502–510.

Ochnser, K. N. & Gross J. J. (2005). The cognitive control of emotion. *Trends in Cognitive Sciences, 9*(5), 242- 249.

Ochner, K.N. & Gross, J. J. (2008). Cognitive Emotion Regulation: Insights From Social Cognitive and Affective Neuroscience. *Current Directions in Psychological Science, 17*(2), 153-158.

Panksepp, J. (1998). *Affective neuroscience: The foundations of human and animal emotions.* New York, N.Y.: Oxford University Press.

Stein, N. L., Leventhal, B., Trabasso, T. (1990). *Psychological and biological approaches to emotion.* Hillsday, New Jersey :Lawrence Erlbaum Associates Inc.

Tomkins, S. S. (1984). Affect theory. In P. Ekman (Ed.) *Emotion in the human face* (2nd ed., pp.
353- 395). New York: Cambridge University Press.

Zajonc, R. B. (1980). Feeling and thinking: Preferences need no inferences. *American
Psychologist, 35,* 151-176.